W9-BZV-852

EXPLORE
my world

Honey Bees

Jill Esbaum

NATIONAL
GEOGRAPHIC
KiDS

WASHINGTON, D.C.

Look, a honey bee!

Buzzing through a warm afternoon, a little worker bee dips into colorful flowers again ... and again ... and again.

A honey bee visits hundreds of flowers a day, tasting each one with its feet!

From each flower, she collects a sweet liquid called nectar.

She sips the runny nectar through her straw-like tongue and stores it in a special, just-for-honey tummy.

The tongue is called a proboscis (pro-bohs-kis).

7

Flower pollen dusts the
bee like fluffy golden snow.

Every once in a while she stops, rolls the pollen into balls, and stuffs these into tiny sacs on her back legs.

Honey, I'm home!

When the bee is so heavy with nectar and pollen she can barely fly, she heads home to the hive.

Thousands of other workers are arriving home, too.

Inside the hive, the air hums with excitement. Bees bustle to and fro.

The whole colony works together for its queen. As long as she is safe and healthy, so is the hive.

Worker bees bring her food and carry out her waste. They fan their wings to keep the hive cool.

A hive is made up of many honeycombs!

One of the most important jobs in the hive is caring for the queen's many eggs.

honey bee egg

Through spring and summer, she lays up to 2,000 eggs per day. She wiggles her abdomen down into a honeycomb and drops each egg into its own six-walled cell.

larva

An egg's shell melts away,
and ... hello, larva!

The chubby baby looks
nothing like a bee. Yet.

For three days, the larva is fed a milky mush called royal jelly. Then it is switched to a honey-pollen mixture called bee bread.

Each larva weaves a cocoon. Inside, its body keeps growing and changing.

Crawl!

Finally, a honey bee chews open its cocoon and climbs out of its cozy cell. Ta-da!

Honey bees keep their hive clean and neat. So the new bee's first job is to clean her room!

Hives can be found in unusual places.

Many honey bees live in human-made hives. A beekeeper opens a hive to remove part of the sticky golden honey. Yum!

Bye-bye, buzzy!

Hope you find a lot of lovely flowers!

Busy as a Bee!

There is plenty of work to do in a honey bee hive. Every worker does each of these jobs in order, moving from one to the next every few days during her six weeks of life.

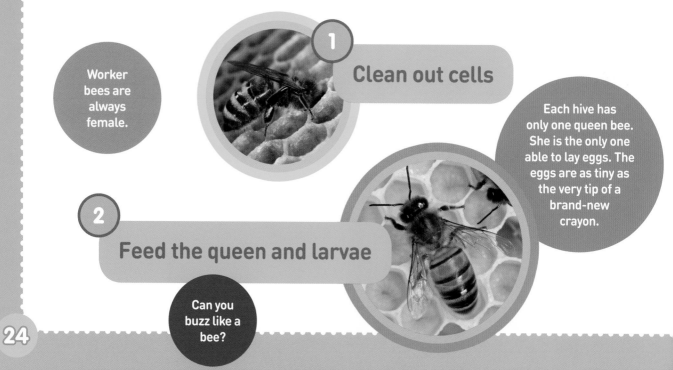

Worker bees are always female.

1 Clean out cells

Each hive has only one queen bee. She is the only one able to lay eggs. The eggs are as tiny as the very tip of a brand-new crayon.

2 Feed the queen and larvae

Can you buzz like a bee?

What is one chore you do at home?

3 Build and repair honeycombs

4 Make honey from nectar

5 Guard the hive entrance

6 Fly out to collect nectar

Have you ever seen a bee on a flower?

Male honey bees, called drones, do not work in the hive and only live long enough to mate with the queen. When fall arrives and the weather turns cold, drones are kicked out of the hive!

Do flowers grow near your home or school?

More Honey, Please!

Bees make honey from flower nectar. They store it in the topmost cells of their honeycomb. They eat both honey and pollen.

Pollen is stored in cells below the honey.

Where do you store your food?

Pollen cells are built above those filled with eggs and growing larvae.

In one day, a worker bee brings home enough nectar to make only a tiny bit of honey. But a hive might have 50,000 or more bees. Working together, they can make as much as two pounds (1 kg) of honey per day. That's enough honey to fill two canning jars.

Do you weigh more or less than two pounds (1 kg)?

What's your favorite sweet treat?

The Bee Is the Key

When bees fly from flower to flower, tiny grains of pollen stick to their feet, then get dropped off on another flower. That's called pollination, and it's what helps flowers make more flowers. Bees pollinate many food crops, too.

salvia plant

28

Without bees, we couldn't enjoy things like apples, blueberries, cherries, cucumbers, strawberries, or melons.

Have you ever picked apples from a tree?

Bees are important to many ecosystems. You can help them by planting nectar-rich flowers like daisies and marigolds, and blue flowers like salvia. Bees seem to like the color blue! You might also plant any of the fruits or berries mentioned above, as well as broccoli, pumpkins, and tomatoes.

What's your favorite vegetable?

Bee Maze

Help the honey bee find its way
back to the hive!

Waggle Dance

When a worker bee returns to the hive, it sometimes does a waggle dance. The special wiggle-waggle moves are actually directions that show other workers where to go to find flowers! Can you look at the picture and waggle dance like a honey bee?

For Hugo and Fiona
—JE

We chose to spell "honey bee" as two words to respect the scientific community's preference. For spelling bee purposes, please note that Merriam-Webster's dictionary spells it as one word, "honeybee."

Copyright © 2017 National Geographic Partners, LLC
Published by National Geographic Partners, LLC,
Washington, D.C. 20036

All rights reserved. Reproduction of the whole or any part of the contents without written permission from the publisher is prohibited.

Since 1888, the National Geographic Society has funded more than 12,000 research, exploration, and preservation projects around the world. The Society receives funds from National Geographic Partners, LLC, funded in part by your purchase. A portion of the proceeds from this book supports this vital work. To learn more, visit www.natgeo.com/info.

NATIONAL GEOGRAPHIC and Yellow Border Design are trademarks of the National Geographic Society, used under license.

Trade paperback ISBN: 978-1-4263-2713-1
Reinforced library binding ISBN: 978-1-4263-2714-8

The publisher gratefully acknowledges bee educator and beekeeper Louise Edsall for her expert review of the book.

Art director and designer: Sanjida Rashid

Printed in the United States of America
22/WOR/6

ILLUSTRATIONS CREDITS
Front cover, anat chant/Shutterstock; Back cover (LO LE), Mrs/Getty Images; 1 (CTR), Musat/Getty Images; 2–3 (CTR), Horst Sollinger/Getty Images; 4–5 (CTR), Photographer/Shutterstock; 6 (UP LE), Dookfish/Getty Images; 7 (CTR), DanielPrudek/Getty Images; 8-9 (CTR), NaturlmDetail/Getty Images; 9 (CTR), Sumiko Scott/Getty Images; 10 (UP), Serg_Velusceac/Getty Images; 10 (LO), Rambynas/Getty Images; 11 (CTR), bo1982/Getty Images; 12 (CTR), satephoto/Shutterstock; 13 (UP), bluedog studio/Shutterstock; 13 (LO), Steve Hopkin/Getty Images; 14 (UP LE), Kerstin Klaassen/Getty Images; 14 (LO RT), Wildlife/Alamy; 15 (CTR), Paul Starosta/Getty Images; 16 (CTR), NinaHenry/Getty Images; 17 (LO), Wildlife/Alamy; 17 (CTR), Taigi/Shutterstock; 18 (UP), Ingo Arndt/Nature Picture Library; 18 (LO), Phil Savoie/Nature Picture Library; 19 (CTR), Jonathan Wilkins/Science Source; 20–21 (CTR), Louis-Laurent Grandadam/Getty Images; 21 (UP RT), S and D and K Maslowski/Minden Pictures; 21 (LO LE), Dionisvera/Shutterstock; 22–23 (CTR), SumikoPhoto/Getty Images; 24 (CTR), Visuals Unlimited, Inc./Robert Pickett/Getty Images; 24 (LO), Simon Colmer/Minden Pictures; 25 (UP), Kenneth H. Thomas/Science Photo Library; 25 (CTR LE), Jonathan Wilkins/Science Photo Library; 25 (CTR RT), temmuz can arsiray/Getty Images; 25 (LO LE), kowit sitthi/Shutterstock; 25 (LO RT), image broker/Alamy; 26 (LE), Susan Schmitz/Shutterstock; 26 (RT), Dionisvera/Shutterstock; 27 (UP), John Burke/Getty Images; 27 (LO), Zerbor/Shutterstock; 28 (LE), Steve Cukrov/Shutterstock; 28 (RT), structuresxx/Getty Images; 29 (UP RT), Kheng Ho Toh/Dreamstime.com; 29 (LO LE), Anna Sedneva/Shutterstock; 29 (LO), Nattika/Shutterstock; 30 (UP), Serg_Velusceac/Getty Images; 30 (LO), fpwing/Getty Images; 31 (CTR), Simon Colmer/Minden Pictures; 32 (UP), Ed Reschke/Getty Images